Level 1

Fold-N-Go Grammar Pack

by Nancy I. Sanders

WriteShop Junior Level 1 Fold-N-Go Grammar Pack
© 2011 by Nancy I. Sanders.
Published and distributed by Demme Learning

This material is to be used in conjunction with WriteShop Junior Book D Teacher's Guide.

All rights reserved. No part of this book may be reproduced, stored in a retrieval system, or transmitted in any form by any means—electronic, mechanical, photocopying, recording, or otherwise—without prior written permission from Demme Learning.

writeshop.com

1-888-854-6284 or +1 717-283-1448 | demmelearning.com
Lancaster, Pennsylvania USA

ISBN 978-1-60826-663-0
Revision Code 0122

Printed in the United States of America by The P.A. Hutchison Company
 2 3 4 5 6 7 8 9 10

For information regarding CPSIA on this printed material call: 1-888-854-6284 and provide reference #0122-01142022

Fold-N-Go™ Grammar

Introduction

Though *Fold-N-Go Grammar*™ is not a complete grammar curriculum, you may find that it helps your child acquire many grammar skills he needs to write successfully at this level. If so, by all means use the guides as your main resource for teaching grammar skills. However, if he struggles to learn the rules about punctuation, sentence structure, or other writing skills, use *Fold-N-Go Grammar* to supplement a more complete grammar program.

Fold-N-Go Grammar is a required component of WriteShop Junior. Even if you are not teaching WriteShop Junior, you can still use *Fold-N-Go Grammar* as an independent resource. Either way, each *Fold-N-Go* helps review or introduce key grammar and writing rules in a fun and engaging way.

Level 1 Fold-N-Go Grammar Pack - Contents

Make the Fold-N-Go

Complete the Activities

Store the Fold-N-Go

Grammar Lessons

- Lesson 1   Punctuation Marks
- Lesson 2   Self-editing
- Lesson 3   Nouns
- Lesson 4   Pronouns
- Lesson 5   Verbs
- Lesson 6   Adjectives
- Lesson 7   Adverbs
- Lesson 8   Prepositions
- Lesson 9   Capitalization
- Lesson 10   References

Answer Keys

Make the Fold-N-Go

This pack will produce 10 unique *Fold-N-Go* grammar guides, six pages each. The pages are designed to be stapled together and affixed inside a file folder to form a large flipbook. If you're teaching more than one child, make one for each student.

Each *Fold-N-Go* is assembled in exactly the same way. Put them together yourself or enlist your child's help.

Gather Supplies

- 10 letter-size manila or colored file folders or a set of 10 fancy file folders.
- Stapler
- Clear packing tape and clear circle stickers (optional)

Prepare the Pages

1. From the Level 1 Fold-N-Go Grammar Pack, remove the six pages for the current lesson's *Fold-N-Go*.
2. Identify the correct page number of each page as shown (figure 1).

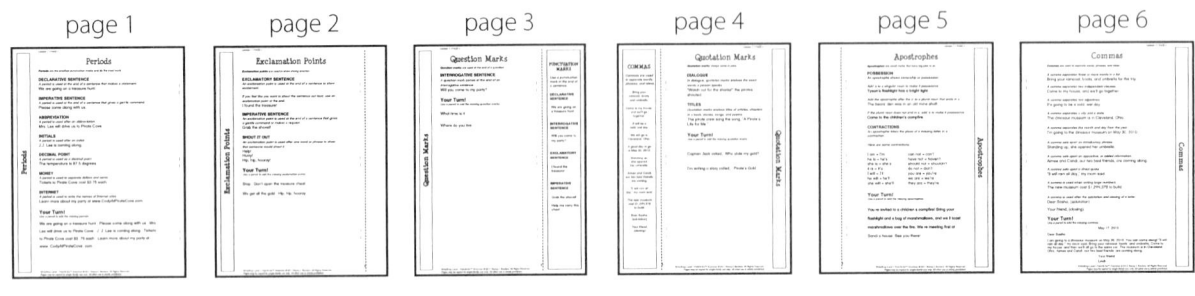

figure 1

3. Cut along the dotted lines on pages 2 and 5 (figure 2).
4. Cut along the dotted lines on pages 3 and 4 as shown (figure 3).
5. Trim the two bookmarks and laminate if desired (figure 4).

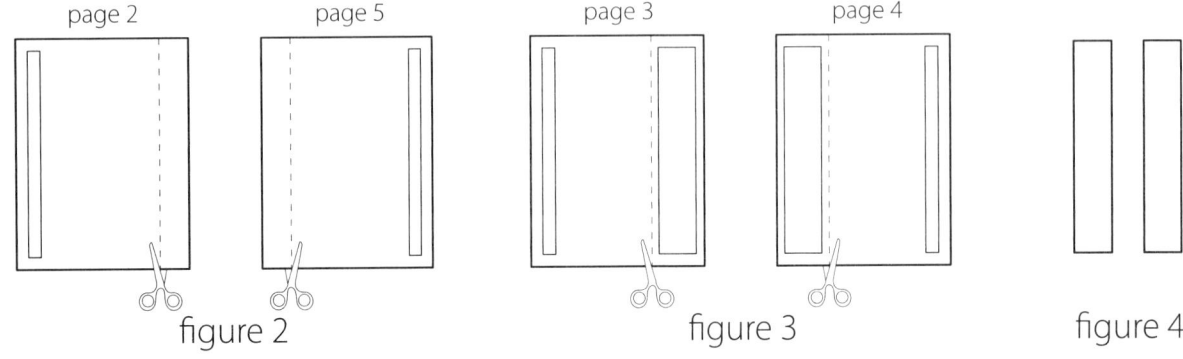

figure 2   figure 3   figure 4

Assemble the Fold-N-Go

1. Stack pages 1, 2, and 3 as shown so that their right edges align together. The left edges should be offset from each other and clearly show the titles of each page (figure 5). Staple them together along the right edges with three staples as shown (figure 6).

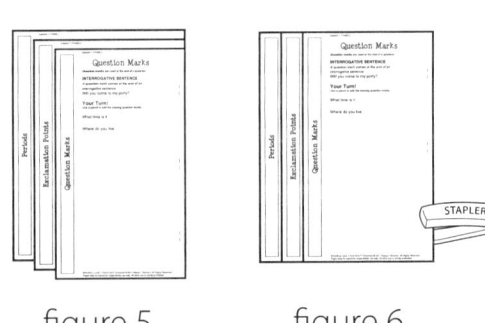

figure 5   figure 6

2. Stack pages 4, 5, and 6 as shown so that their left edges align together. The right edges should be offset from each other and clearly show the titles of each page (figure 7). Staple them together along the left edges with three staples as shown (figure 8).

3. Staple the stack of pages 1, 2, and 3 to the left side of the inside of the file folder along the top and bottom of page 1 as shown (figure 9). Do *not* staple all three pages. Only page 1 will be stapled to the folder. Alternatively, you may tape or glue page 1 in place.

4. Staple the stack of pages 4, 5, and 6 to the right side of the inside of the file folder along the top and bottom of page 6 as shown (figure 10). Do *not* staple all three pages. Only page 6 will be stapled to the folder. Alternatively, you may tape or glue page 6 in place.

5. For durability, tape a strip of clear packing tape down the center of the file folder to cover the staples (figure 11). On the outside, affix a clear circle sticker over each staple to avoid scratching or catching on clothes (figure 12).

6. On both the tab and front of the folder, write the name of the *Fold-N-Go*. Let your child decorate the cover, if desired.

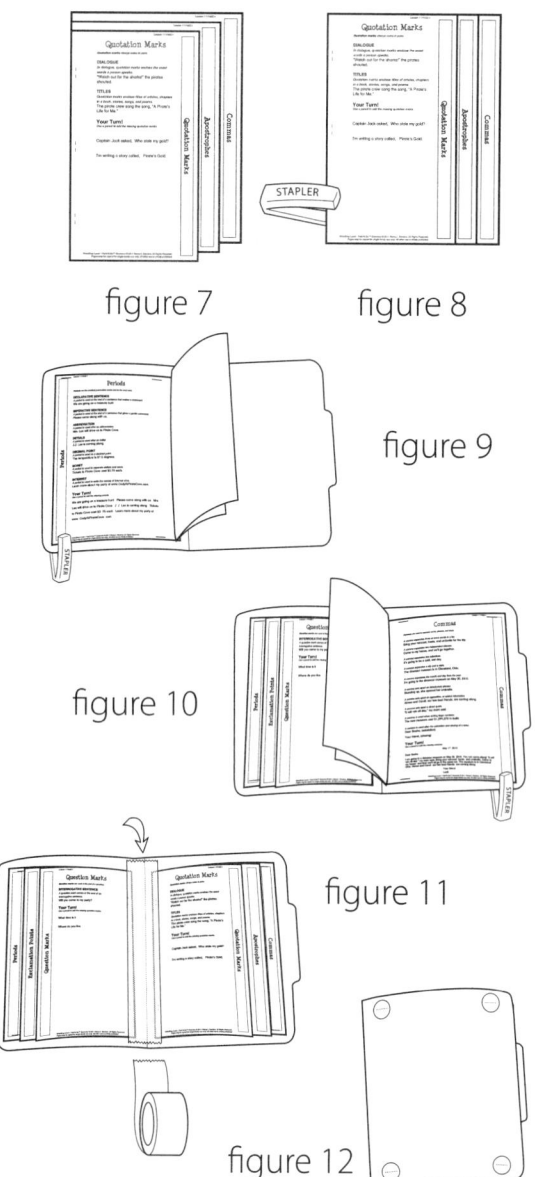

figure 7   figure 8

figure 9

figure 10

figure 11

figure 12

Make the Bookmarks

Along with each *Fold-N-Go* grammar guide, you will cut out two bookmarks that highlight the lesson's grammar or writing skills at a glance.

1. For durability, laminate the bookmarks or glue them on cardstock. Consider gluing or laminating them back-to-back to form one bookmark for each writing skill.

2. Store these in a jar in the writing center. Keep them handy so your child can pull the bookmarks out and refresh his memory about grammar rules during writing or editing.

3. You may also choose to tape or glue these inside a file folder as a quick reference. Use one file folder to store bookmarks from Lessons 1-5 and another to store bookmarks from Lessons 6-10. Label the covers and tabs accordingly (figure 13).

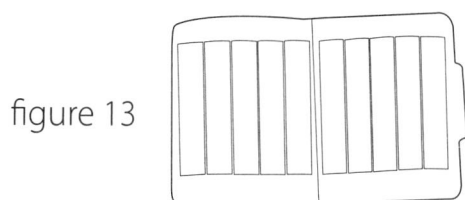

figure 13

Complete the Activities

When to Do Fold-N-Go Activities

WriteShop Junior Students: If you are using WriteShop Junior Book D, each lesson will instruct you to assemble and complete a new Fold-N-Go together with your child. Because most Fold-N-Gos are directly related to their corresponding lessons, your child will benefit from making and using each one as it is assigned (see Book D Teacher's Guide). Even if he is eager and enthusiastic, it's best to keep your child on schedule and not let him jump ahead to the other Fold-N-Gos until they are assigned.

All Other Students: If you are using the Level 1 Fold-N-Go Grammar Pack as a stand-alone grammar resource, feel free to work at your own pace. Or, make one Fold-N-Go every week for 10 weeks according to this schedule:

Day 1: Assemble the Fold-N-Go

Day 2: Pages 1 and 2

Day 3: Pages 3 and 4

Day 4: Pages 5 and 6

How to Do Fold-N-Go Activities

1. Open the *Fold-N-Go* so you and your student can easily see all six pages at a glance.
2. Read through each page together, allowing time for your child to complete the pencil activities. Do not let him use a pen for these exercises.
3. After each pencil activity, discuss his answers. (An answer key is provided in the back of the Level 1 Fold-N-Go Grammar Pack.)
4. If he makes a mistake, praise him for his efforts. Offer gentle correction and erase the mistake or help him use correction tape before having him write the correct answer.
5. Because this guide will be used in future lessons as a point of reference, it's important to answer each pencil activity correctly. As an option, your child may dictate the correct answer for you to write down.

When finished, check your child's responses against the Answer Key in the back of the Fold-N-Go Grammar Pack. If the material is new to him and it was a challenge to learn, plan on re-teaching this topic and practicing this skill during future sessions.

Store the Fold-N-Go

One of the purposes of *Fold-N-Go Grammar* is to create a handy resource for your child to refer to during the writing and editing process. Therefore, keep each folder easily accessible in your writing area. Here are some storage suggestions.

- File drawer in your child's desk
- 3.5-inch accordion-style letter-size file pocket
- File box for holding letter-size file folders

Commas

Commas *are used to separate words, phrases, and ideas.*

A comma separates three or more words in a list.
Bring your raincoat, boots, and umbrella for the trip.

A comma separates two independent clauses.
Come to my house, and we'll go together.

A comma separates two adjectives.
It's going to be a cold, wet day.

A comma separates a city and a state.
The dinosaur museum is in Cleveland, Ohio.

A comma separates the month and day from the year.
I'm going to the dinosaur museum on May 30, 2010.

A comma sets apart an introductory phrase.
Standing up, she opened her umbrella.

A comma sets apart an appositive, or added information.
Aimee and Candi, our two best friends, are coming along.

A comma is used after the salutation and closing of a letter.
Dear Sasha, (salutation)

Your friend, (closing)

Your Turn!
Use a pencil to add the missing commas.

May 17 2014

Dear Grandpa

    I went to a dinosaur museum in Blanding Utah. Lucy my neighbor had never been there before. She loved it! We saw fossils skeletons and footprints. There was a gift shop and we bought postcards. Later we had a picnic at a shady beautiful park. Lucy and I had a lot of fun.

                      Your grandson

                      Henry

Content

When you self-edit your writing, work to improve these areas:

Write a strong beginning.

Develop the middle.

Write a satisfying end.

Develop the main idea by adding details, examples, and descriptions.

Focus your writing.

Check that your writing makes sense.

Your Turn!
Use a pencil to fill in the blanks.

Superheroes know that power-packed writing has:

A strong _____.

A developed _____.

A satisfying _____.

Self-editing Check

*Use a **self-editing checklist** to help you find ways to improve your writing.*

☐ I used proofreading marks to make corrections.

☐ I indented each new paragraph.

☐ I wrote complete sentences.

☐ I started each sentence with a capital letter.

☐ I ended each sentence with a period, question mark, or exclamation point.

☐ I used a capital letter for each proper noun.

☐ I checked that I used commas correctly.

☐ I looked in a dictionary to check my spelling.

☐ I looked in a thesaurus to find strong words.

Your Turn!
Use a pencil to write your answers.

The marks I make on my paper to correct my mistakes are called __proofreading__ __marks__. I look in a __dictionary__ to check my spelling, and I look in a __thesaurus__ to find strong words.

Lesson 2 Self-editing | PAGE 3

Proofreading Marks A

Mark	What It Means	Sample
≡	change to a capital letter	<u>s</u>uperball <u>g</u>irl can bounce all the way to <u>m</u>ars.
lc/	change to a lower case letter	She bounces over ˡᶜ/Mountains.
SP	write correct spelling	Rubberband Boy stretches to the moone.⒮ᴾ
∽	delete	Their superpowers are ~~are~~ super amazing.
⌒	delete space	Every⌒thing Eraser Kid touches turns invisible.
#	insert space	He can#also race really fast.
⊙	insert period	Together they can save their town⊙They can even save the world.

Your Turn!

Use a pencil to edit and add the proofreading marks.

superball Girl bounces over hills. Eraser Kid turns every thing invisible. They they areamazing.

Proofreading Marks

change to a capital letter

change to a lowercase letter

write correct spelling

delete

delete space

insert space

⊙
insert period

Lesson 2 Self-editing | PAGE 4

Proofreading Marks

¶
start a new paragraph

∧
insert here

∧̣
insert comma

⟨⟨∧ ∧⟩⟩
insert quotation marks

?∧
insert question mark

!∧
insert exclamation point

∼
reverse letters or words

Proofreading Marks B

Mark	What It Means	Sample
¶	start new paragraph	They're great! ¶One day they became friends.
∧	insert here	Each day, they look for people ∧to help.
∧̣	insert comma	They help babies∧ little children∧ and grandmas.
⟨⟨∧ ∧⟩⟩	insert quotation marks	∧Help! Help!∧ cries Julio.
?∧	insert question mark	Will someone come to help?∧ Julio needs help now.
!∧	insert exclamation point	Hip, hip, hooray!∧ Rubberband Boy saves the day.
∼	reverse letters or words	Thank for you speeding to the rescue.

Your Turn!

Use a pencil to edit and add the proofreading marks.

Superheroes look for babies children adn grandmas help.

Help   cries Julio.

Proofreading Marks B

Self-editing Tools

DICITIONARY

Use a dictionary to check the spelling of hard words.

Make your own dictionary of commonly misspelled words.

THESAURUS

A thesaurus is a book that lists **synonyms** (words that mean the same) and **antonyms** (words that mean the opposite) of many different words.

Use a thesaurus to help choose strong words like **descriptive adjectives** and **action verbs**.

Your Turn!
Look in your thesaurus. Use a pencil to write down five synonyms for the word "run."

1. _____
2. _____
3. _____
4. _____
5. _____

Self-editing Tips

HAVE FUN!

Try to make editing like playing a game. Pretend you have superpowers and can spot mistakes a mile away!

Wear a special Editor's Hat while you edit.

Start by looking for a difficult word you spelled correctly and a perfect sentence you wrote.

Highlight both with a highlighter, or give yourself a sticker for each. Good job!

To find misspelled words, start at the bottom and read backwards, word by word.

To find incomplete sentences, read your story backwards, sentence by sentence.

Your Turn!
Use a pencil to write your answer.

Which self-editing tip sounds like the most fun?

_____

_____

_____ .

I Know Nouns!

Nouns are words that name a person, place, or thing.

Jessica and **Noah** packed their **suitcases** for their **trip** to **Pluto**. Their pet **monkey** is coming, too.

In her suitcase, Jessica packed:
a **toothbrush**
her **hairbrush**
a clean **washcloth**

In his suitcase, Noah packed:
toys
books
video **games**

In his suitcase, their pet monkey packed:
bananas
an **orange**
his favorite **blanket**

DID YOU KNOW?
Some nouns are common nouns like **monkey** and **bananas**.
Some nouns are proper nouns like **Jessica** and **Pluto**.

Your Turn!
Use a pencil to write a list of nouns that name things you would pack in your suitcase if you were blasting off in a rocket ship to Pluto. Choose at least one proper noun.

_____   _____

_____   _____

_____   _____

_____   _____

Common and Proper Nouns

COMMON NOUNS
Common nouns do not name a particular person, place, or thing.

girl
state
day
month
holiday

PROPER NOUNS
Proper nouns describe the name of a particular person, place, day of the week, month, or holiday.

Alex Noonan
Pennsylvania
Monday
December
Kwanzaa

Your Turn!
Use a pencil to write a proper noun on the blank that can be used in place of each common noun.

A girl and boy blast off in their rocket to land on a planet. They will fly back to their town next month.

girl _____

boy _____

rocket _____

planet _____

town _____

month _____

Collective Nouns

Collective nouns are a special kind of noun.
A collective noun names a group of people, places, or things.

bunch of flowers
pile of sticks
string of pearls
bag of potatoes
row of seats

DID YOU KNOW?
Different collective nouns can describe different groups of people.

audience	department
class	family
committee	jury
company	team

DID YOU KNOW?
Different collective nouns are used to describe specific groups of animals.

colony of ants   **herd** of cows
hive of bees   **pack** of wolves
flock of birds   **pride** of lions
litter of kittens   **school** of fish

Your Turn!
Use a pencil to draw a line to connect the collective noun with the group it describes.

class	of deer
flock	of porpoises
herd	of children
team	of turkeys
school	of players

Common and Proper Nouns

COMMON NOUNS
Common nouns do not name a particular person, place, or thing.

girl
state
day
month
holiday

PROPER NOUNS
Proper nouns describe the name of a particular person, place, day of the week, month, or holiday.

Alex Noonan
Pennsylvania
Monday
December
Kwanzaa

I Know Nouns!

Nouns are words that name a person, place, or thing.

PLURAL NOUNS
Singular nouns name one thing.

Plural nouns name more than one.

RULE:
Most singular nouns change to plural by adding -s.

rocket → rockets

RULE:
Add -es when a noun ends in ch, sh, s, ss, x, z, or zz.

lunch → lunches

RULE:
For nouns that end in a consonant followed by a -y, change the y to i and add -es.

guppy → guppies

RULE:
For many nouns that end in -f or -fe, change the f to v and add -es.

shelf → shelves

IRREGULAR NOUNS
Some nouns change to plural in irregular ways.

mouse → mice

Some nouns do not change at all.

moose → moose

Plural Nouns: Add -s or -es

*A singular noun is one person, place, or thing. When there are two or more, write the **plural noun**.*

DID YOU KNOW?
There are rules for changing singular nouns into plural nouns.

RULE: Add -s
Most nouns change into plural nouns by adding -s.

one rocket, two or more **rockets**
one spacesuit, two or more **spacesuits**
one glove, two or more **gloves**

RULE: Add -es
When a noun ends in ch, sh, s, ss, x, z, or zz, add -es.

one fox, two or more **foxes**
one wrench, two **wrenches**
one compass, two or more **compasses**

Your Turn!
*Use a pencil to write **-s** or **-es** on the blanks to change the singular nouns into plural nouns.*

Jessica and Noah are junior astronaut_____. They grab their helmet_____ out of their box_____. They pull on their glove_____ and pack their lunch_____. Now they are ready to blast off and plant two flag_____ on Pluto!

Plural Nouns: Change the Letter

*When changing from singular to plural, some nouns **change the last letter** before adding **-es**.*

RULE: Change the *y* to *i*
For nouns that end in a consonant followed by a *-y*, change the *y* to *i* and add *-es*.

one diary, two or more **diaries**
one baby, two or more **babies**
one kitty, two or more **kitties**

DID YOU KNOW?
For nouns that end in a vowel followed by a -y, just add -s.

one day, two or more **days**
one key, two or more **keys**
one monkey, two or more **monkeys**

RULE: Change the *f* to *v*
For many (not all) nouns that end in *-f* or *-fe*, change the *f* to *v* and add *-es*.

one shelf, two or more **shelves**
one knife, two or more **knives**
one loaf, two or more **loaves**

Your Turn!
Use a pencil to circle the correct spelling of the plural nouns.

Jessica and Noah write in their **diarys / diaries** about their trip to Pluto. On their trip, they are bringing three **guppies / guppys** named Frank, Goldilocks, and Penelope. The **shelfs / shelves** inside the rocket are full, so the fish tank floats in the air.

Plural Nouns: Irregular

PLURAL NOUNS: IRREGULAR
Some singular nouns change in unpredictable ways when they become plural.

one goose, two or more **geese**
one mouse, two or more **mice**
one woman, two or more **women**
one child, two or more **children**

DID YOU KNOW?
Some singular nouns do not change at all when they become plural. They stay the same.

one moose, two or more **moose**
one bison, two or more **bison**
one sheep, two or more **sheep**

Your Turn!
Use a pencil to circle the correct spelling of the plural nouns.

Jessica and Noah have two **sheep / sheeps** inside the rocket. And

surprise! Three **mouses / mice** have sneaked on board. When they

land their rocket ship, Jessica and Noah will be the first

child / children to walk on Pluto!

I Know Pronouns!

Pronouns are words that take the place of nouns.

DID YOU KNOW?
A pronoun can also take the place of a group of words called a noun phrase.

Tatum found a bag of seeds.
She found **it**.

Tatum planted a seed.
She planted **it**.

A tree grew in Tatum's yard.
It grew in **her** yard.

The tree grew bigger than Tatum's family's house.
It grew bigger than **their** house.

Soon Tatum's friends came to see the giant tree.
Soon **everyone** came to see **it**.

Did Tatum's friends want to plant a seed?
Did **anybody** want to plant **one**?

Your Turn!
Use a pencil to underline the pronouns.

She told them it was a wishing tree.

It could grow bikes and toys and candy.

It could grow anything they wished!

Singular or Plural Pronouns

*Some pronouns are **singular** and some are **plural**, just like the nouns they replace.*

A bike helmet grew on the wishing tree.
It grew on the wishing tree.

A scooter grew on the very top branch.
It grew on the very top branch.

Bryant stood underneath the wishing tree and wished for candy.
He stood underneath **it** and wished for candy.

Lollipops grew on each branch.
They grew on each branch.

Tatum handed out lollipops to her friends.
She handed out lollipops to **them**.

Bryant got a lollipop, too.
He got **one**, too.

DID YOU KNOW?
You can be a singular pronoun OR a plural pronoun, depending on the noun it replaces.

"Does Bryant want a lollipop?" Tatum asked.
"Do **you** want a lollipop?" Tatum asked.

"Do my friends want lollipops?" Tatum asked.
"Do **you** want lollipops?" Tatum asked.

Your Turn!
Use a pencil to circle the correct pronouns.

Tatum gave candy bars to all **their / her** friends.

Bryant ate **his / their** candy bar right away.

Tatum's friends ate **their / hers** candy bars, too.

Male or Female Pronouns

*Some **pronouns are male or female**, just like the nouns they replace.*

DID YOU KNOW?
***He**, **him**, and **his** are male pronouns.*
***She**, **her**, and **hers** are female pronouns.*

Tatum liked Tatum's wishing tree.
She liked **her** wishing tree.

Tatum's friend Rhiannon wanted a wishing tree, too.
She wanted a wishing tree, too.

So did the President of the United States!
So did **he**!

Tatum gave Rhiannon a seed.
She gave **her** a seed.

Tatum gave the President a seed to plant in the President's yard, too.
She gave **him** a seed to plant in **his** yard, too.

Your Turn!
Use a pencil to circle the female pronouns. Then underline the male pronouns.

Rhiannon planted her seed. A giant wishing tree grew up in her back yard. The President took his seed back to the White House. He planted the seed in his yard. He soon had a giant wishing tree, too.

I Know Pronouns!

Pronouns are words that take the place of nouns.

Tatum planted a seed.
She planted **it**.

MALE OR FEMALE PRONOUNS
Some pronouns are male or female, just like the nouns they replace.

Tatum gave Bryant a seed.
She gave **him** a seed.

SINGULAR OR PLURAL PRONOUNS
Some pronouns are singular and some are plural, just like the nouns they replace.

Gumballs grew on a branch.
They grew on **it**.

Personal Pronouns

replace the name of the person or people you are writing about.

I	me
he	him
she	her
it	
we	us
they	them
you	

DID YOU KNOW?
A personal pronoun can replace a proper or a common noun.

Jo made a wish.
She made a wish.

The boy planted a seed.
He planted it.

Possessive Pronouns

show ownership.

my	mine
his	
her	hers
its	
our	ours
their	theirs

Bryant planted a bush.
The bush was **his**.

DID YOU KNOW?
Apostrophes change meaning.

It's means **it is**.
It's is not possessive.

Jobs Pronouns Do

*Different pronouns have different **jobs to do**.*

INTERROGATIVE PRONOUNS
help ask a question.

what, which, who, whom, whose
whatever, whichever, whoever, whomever

Who will get a wish from the wishing tree?

DEMONSTRATIVE PRONOUNS
help point to where an item is.

this, that, these, those

Those are Tatum's seeds.

INDEFINITE PRONOUNS
talk about nouns that aren't specific people, places, or things.

another, anybody, anyone, anything, each, either, everybody, everyone, everything, neither, nobody, nothing, one, somebody, someone, something, both, few, many, several, all, any, none, some

Tatum invites **everyone** to make a wish on the wishing tree!

Your Turn!
Use a pencil to draw a line to match the pronoun with its job.

what   demonstrative pronoun

this   indefinite pronoun

nobody   interrogative pronoun

Personal Pronouns

*A **personal pronoun** is used to replace the name of the person or people you are writing about.*

I	me
he	him
she	her
it	
we	us
they	them
you	

DID YOU KNOW?
A personal pronoun can replace a proper noun or a common noun.

Jo made a wish on the wishing tree.
She made a wish on the wishing tree.

The boy made a wish, too.
He made a wish, too.

DID YOU KNOW?
A personal pronoun can also be used to replace the name of an animal.

Mittens wished for more cat food to eat.
She wished for more cat food to eat.

DID YOU KNOW?
There are lots of pronouns, but personal pronouns are the ones you use the most.

Your Turn!
Use a pencil to write down the personal pronouns after you unscramble the letters in each word.

em = _____   rhe = _____   etyh = _____

oyu = _____   eh = _____   esh = _____

Possessive Pronouns

A *possessive pronoun* tells who owns something.

Singular possessive pronouns: my, mine, her, hers, his, its
Plural possessive pronouns: our, ours, your, yours, their, theirs

Tatum found another bag of seeds.
The seeds were **hers**.

Tatum gave a seed to me.
The seed was **mine**.

Tatum's friends planted seeds, too. Each seed grew into a bush.
The bushes were **theirs**.

Eating the bush's fruit will turn you invisible!
Eating **its** fruit will turn you invisible!

DID YOU KNOW?
Adding an apostrophe changes a word's meaning.
The word **its** shows ownership. **Its** is a possessive pronoun.
The word **it's** means **it is**. **It's** is *not* a possessive pronoun.

The bush's fruit tastes sweet.
Its fruit tastes sweet.

The fruit is sweet.
It is sweet.
It's sweet.

Your Turn!
Use a pencil to circle the correct possessive pronoun.

These are Tatum's seeds.
These are **her / their** seeds.

This bush belongs to Jo and me.
This is **our / their** bush.

Special fruit grew on the bush's branches.
Special fruit grew on **it's / its** branches.

Lesson 4 Pronouns | PAGE 6

Possessive Pronouns

Action Verbs

Verbs are words that show action or a state of being.

DID YOU KNOW?
Most verbs show action.

Tater Alligator **stomps** through the town.

He **hunts** for potatoes.

DID YOU KNOW?
Some sentences have two or more verbs.

Tater Alligator **steals** everyone's potatoes and **gobbles** them down.

DID YOU KNOW?
A sentence can just be one word if it is a verb.

Stop!
Hurry!
Run!

DID YOU KNOW?
The tense of a verb shows when an action happens.

Past tense shows an action happening **in the past**.

Present tense shows an action happening **right now**.

Future tense shows an action happening **in the future**.

Your Turn!
Use a pencil to circle the action verbs.

Tater Alligator digs up tiny potatoes from the field.

He grabs potatoes at the restaurant.

All day long, he chomps on potatoes.

Present Tense Verbs

Present tense shows action that is happening right now, in the present.

Here are examples of present tense.

Look out! Here **comes** Tater Alligator.

He **visits** the bakery, but there **are** no potatoes.

He **stops** at the pet store, but there **are** no potatoes.

He **hurries** into the grocery store, and he **finds** piles of potatoes.

Tater Alligator **eats** every single potato in one gulp!

DID YOU KNOW?
Some verbs do not show much action. These are weak verbs. Some verbs show a lot of exciting action. These are strong verbs. You can choose to use strong verbs when you write!

Weak Verb: Tater Alligator **gets** the potatoes.
Strong Verb: Tater Alligator **grabs** the potatoes.

Weak Verb: Tater Alligator **goes** through the town.
Strong Verb: Tater Alligator **wanders** through the town.

Your Turn!
Use a pencil to circle the present tense verb that shows what is happening right now.

Tater Alligator **stomped / stomps** into the restaurant.

He **nibble / nibbles** all the french fries.

Tater Alligator **looks / look** for sweet potatoes, too.

Linking Verbs

Some verbs connect—or link—the subject to more information about the subject. **Linking verbs** *do not show action. They show a state of being.*

Tater Alligator **is** as big as an elephant.

He **has been** hungry since the day he **was** born.

DID YOU KNOW?
Any form of the verb **be** *is always a linking verb.*

is	am being
am	is being
are	are being
was	have been
were	has been
will be	might have been

Your Turn!
Use a pencil to circle the linking verbs.

Potatoes are a problem for Tater Alligator.

He has been greedy. Now he is too big for his overalls.

They were the right size last week, but now they are too tight.

If he is not careful, soon he will be too big for his favorite pajamas.

I Know Verbs!

Verbs are words that show action or a state of being.

ACTION VERBS

Most verbs show action.

Examples:
climb
shout
write
escape
carve
grow

LINKING VERBS

Some verbs link the subject with more information.

Linking verbs show a state of being.

Any form of the verb **be** *is a linking verb.*

Examples:
is
am
are
was
were
will be
am being
is being
are being
have been
has been
may have been

Past Tense Regular Verbs

Verb Tense

The tense of a verb shows **when** something happens.

PAST TENSE REGULAR VERBS show action happening in the past.

Regular verbs form past tense by adding -d or -ed.

  hike, hiked
  paint, painted
  close, closed

PAST TENSE IRREGULAR VERBS show action happening in the past.

Irregular verbs form past tense in irregular ways.

  build, built
  forget, forgot
  keep, kept

PRESENT TENSE shows action happening right now.

  knows
  freezes
  carries

FUTURE TENSE shows action happening in the future.

  will race
  will hide
  will dive

Past tense shows action that happened in the past. *Regular verbs* are written in past tense by adding **-d** or **-ed**.

Tater Alligator **wanted** more potatoes.

He **stopped** in every town and **looked** for potatoes.

DID YOU KNOW?
Most verbs are regular verbs.

Here is a sample of regular verbs.

PRESENT TENSE	PAST TENSE
march	marched
pop	popped
dance	danced
imagine	imagined
bark	barked
hop	hopped
clean	cleaned
laugh	laughed
jump	jumped
open	opened

Your Turn!

Use a pencil to circle the **past tense regular verbs** you find in this word search. Use the past tense verbs from the list above. Look forward, backward, up, down, and diagonally.

```
D W B A R K E D D X
E T Z A Q Y Z O E M
C L E A N E D L P A
N R J D E P P O P R
A X O Z O W D Q O C
D O Q W Y E J X H H
D E N E P O T R Y E
W Q I M A G I N E D
H X U Z Y X R W B F
K J G L A U G H E D
```

Past Tense Irregular Verbs

Past tense shows action that happened in the past.
Irregular verbs are written in past tense in irregular ways.

Yesterday, Tater Alligator **went** to Melissa's house.

He **took** all her french fries. There **were** none left.

So Melissa **taught** him to share.

She **fed** him half her potato chips and **ate** the other half herself.

Then she **sang** him a silly song about good manners.

After that, he **was** a new alligator!

DID YOU KNOW?
There is no pattern to irregular verbs.
You cannot predict how irregular verbs will change from present tense to past tense.

Here is a sample of irregular verbs.

List #1

PRESENT TENSE	PAST TENSE
go	went
eat	ate
are	were
take	took
feed	fed
sing	sang
is	was
hurt	hurt
win	won
shake	shook

List #2

PRESENT TENSE	PAST TENSE
shut	shut
speak	spoke
see	saw
buy	bought
draw	drew
dig	dug
come	came
bite	bit
do	did
wear	wore

Your Turn!
Use a pencil to circle the past tense irregular verbs.

Last week, Brandon **teaches / taught** Tater Alligator a new trick.

Tater Alligator **sits / sat** on command.

Then Brandon **fed / feeds** him a french fry for a reward.

Future Tense Verbs

Future tense shows action that will happen later, in the future.

We **will see** you later, Tater Alligator!

DID YOU KNOW?
If you add the word "will" before the verb, it changes to future tense:

PRESENT TENSE	**FUTURE TENSE**
stomp	will stomp
grab	will grab
gobble	will gobble

Here are examples of future tense.

Brandon **will show** Tater Alligator a trick tomorrow.
Melissa **will teach** Tater Alligator nice manners next week.
He **will stomp** and he **will chomp**, but soon he **will say** "please" and "thank you."
He **will take** his potatoes politely on a plate.

Your Turn!
Use a pencil to change the verbs to future tense. The first one is done for you.

PRESENT TENSE		**FUTURE TENSE**	
chew	w i l l	c h e w	
try	__ __ __ __	__ __ __ (1)	
count	__ __ __ __	__ __ __ __ __ (2)	
lift	__ __ __ __	__ __ __ __ (3)	
skip	__ __ __ __	__ __ __ __ (4)	

Write the corresponding letter on each blank below to answer this question:

What are Tater Alligator's favorite kind of potatoes?

Tater __ __ __ __ ®
      1 2 3 4

Lesson 5 Verbs | PAGE 6

Where Adjectives Are Found

ADJECTIVES COME BEFORE
In many sentences, an adjective comes right before the noun or pronoun that it describes.

Please come to an **exciting** play!
It is in the **community** theater.
Mariah performs the part of a **wealthy** ballerina.
She wears a **diamond** tiara.
Kirk will play a **sneaky** spy.
He wears a **detective** coat.
Tickets go on sale **next** week.

ADJECTIVES COME AFTER
An adjective can also come after the noun or pronoun that it describes. If the sentence has a linking verb, the adjective often comes after the linking verb.

The spy feels **brave**.
The ballerina looks **angelic**.
The play is **new**.
The tickets are **cheap**.
The audience seems **excited** for the curtain to rise.

Your Turn!
Read each sentence. Write the answers on the blanks.

The nervous actors put on their costumes.

Which adjective describes the actors? _____

The eager audience waits in their seats.

Which adjective describes the audience? _____

Kirk looks sly as he hides in the shadows.

Which adjective describes Kirk? _____

Mariah is lovely in her pink tutu.

Which adjective describes Mariah? _____

Adjectives Compare Things

ONE THING
Some adjectives describe one noun or pronoun.

Kirk uses a **big** magnifying glass because he is an **important** spy.

Mariah wears a **sparkly** tiara because she is **wealthy**.

TWO THINGS
Some adjectives can compare two nouns or pronouns. Adjectives that compare two things end in -er or add the word more.

Kirk's magnifying glass is **bigger** than Craig's magnifying glass because he is **more important** than Craig.

Mariah's tiara is **more sparkly** than Katy's because she is **wealthier** than Katy.

THREE THINGS
Some adjectives can compare three or more nouns or pronouns. Adjectives that compare three things end in -est or add the word most.

Kirk uses the **biggest** magnifying glass because he is the **most important** spy in the play.

Mariah wears the **most sparkly** tiara of all because she is the **wealthiest** of all.

Your Turn!
Use a pencil to circle the correct adjective.

Kirk's hat is **taller / tallest** than Craig's.

Mariah's tutu is the **more pink / most pink** of all.

Mariah dances the **longer / longest** dance of all.

I Know Adjectives!

Adjectives describe nouns and pronouns.

Each **adjective** tells us something different about a person, place, or thing.

Mariah wears a **chartreuse** tutu.
Mariah wears a **fluffy** tutu.
Mariah wears a **fancy** tutu.
It is also **scratchy**.

Kirk acts as a **clever** spy.
Kirk acts as an **obnoxious** spy.
Kirk acts as a **suspicious** spy.
He is **sneaky**.

DID YOU KNOW?
You can choose to use interesting and exciting adjectives when you write!

Your Turn!
Use a pencil to draw a line to connect each noun with an interesting adjective.

NOUN	ADJECTIVE
tiara	leather
helmet	smooth
leotard	dainty
slippers	fuchsia
boots	tough

I Know Adjectives!

ADJECTIVES describe nouns and pronouns.

ADJECTIVES COME BEFORE NOUNS

exciting play
community theater
diamond tiara
sneaky spy

ADJECTIVES COME AFTER LINKING VERBS

The ballerina is **beautiful**.
The spy was **brave**.
The tickets are **cheap**.
The audience feels **excited**.

ADJECTIVES COMPARE

big coat
bigger coat
biggest coat

beautiful tiara
more beautiful tiara
most beautiful tiara

Lesson 6 Adjectives | PAGE 4

Adjectives

ADJECTIVES
tell information about people, places, and things.

SIZE:
thin
short
medium
tall

SHAPE:
round
flat
puffy
spiral

COLOR:
bright green
azure
khaki
violet

AGE:
teenage
young
ancient
fresh

HOW MUCH:
most
three
every
no

You can choose interesting and exciting adjectives when you write!

Lists of Adjectives

*Look for **adjectives** everywhere! Here are some you'll find.*

ADJECTIVES TELL SIZE
giant	long	thick
tiny	low	heavy
medium	average	petite
tall	huge	grand

ADJECTIVES TELL SHAPE
round	square	triangular
diamond	oval	circular
oblong	curved	twisted
spiral	coiled	bent

ADJECTIVES TELL COLOR
lavender	lilac	ivory
plum	khaki	deep red
cerulean	teal	ebony

ADJECTIVES TELL AGE
old	young	original
ancient	new	mature
fresh	stale	antique
elderly	newborn	brand-new

ADJECTIVES TELL HOW MUCH
many	few	enough
twelve	most	great
countless	every	a hundred
all	no	each

Your Turn!
Use a pencil to write your favorite adjectives on the blanks.

Mariah is the _____ ballerina.

She has been in _____ shows.

The tiara is covered with _____ jewels.

Lists of Adjectives

Using Adjectives When We Write

*When we write stories, **adjectives help us** describe people, places, and things.*

THE SETTING
Use adjectives to describe an interesting and exciting setting for your story.

The **large** theater holds **eighty** seats.

We love the **velvet** curtains and the **soft** seats.

The stage can be **slippery**.

There is a **snack** shop outside with **chocolate** pretzels and **buttered** popcorn.

MAIN CHARACTERS
Use adjectives to write important details about your main characters.

Mariah is **talented**, but she is **afraid** of slipping on the stage.

Her **ballet** shoes are **slippery**, too.

She is **careful** when she dances.

Kirk is a **professional** actor.

He is a **television** star.

His **spy** costume feels **itchy**, so he wants to wear a **new** coat.

OTHER CHARACTERS
Use adjectives to write important details about the other characters in your story, too.

Craig is **older** than the other characters.

This is his **fifth** play.

Katy is Kirk's **younger** sister.

She wears **beautiful** costumes.

Your Turn!
Use a pencil to circle the adjectives.

Kirk gets a new coat, but it is baggier than his old coat.

He's grumpy because he can't find the perfect coat.

Using Adjectives in Poetry

*Choosing adjectives carefully can help us write more exciting, meaningful, or beautiful **poetry**.*

HAIKU
A haiku is a type of Japanese poem that has 3 lines and uses 17 syllables: 5 in the first line, 7 in the second line, and 5 in the third line.

The Ballerina
Floating pink flower
Graceful arms, **pointed** toes dance
Delightful music

ACROSTIC
An acrostic is a poem where the first letters in each line spell a word. You can use adjectives on each line to describe the word.

Suspicious detective
Popular sleuth
Yellow coat

OTHER POEMS
Adjectives add color and interest to poems, especially because every word is important in a poem.

An elephant named Frank had a cold.
He was a **silly** sight to behold.
His **big** ears were **spotted**, he had **purple** toes,
And his **long** nose was **red** as a rose.

Your Turn!
Use a pencil to complete the acrostic with as many adjectives as you can.

P_____

E_____

T_____

S_____

Adverbs Answer Questions

Adverbs tell us when, where, how, and how much.
Adverbs answer questions *about verbs.*

WHEN?
Twins Jampo and Kipu hiked up the mountain **today**.
When did they hike? Today!

WHERE?
A mountain goat followed them **everywhere**.
Where did the goat follow them? Everywhere!

HOW?
Jampo and Kipu climbed **carefully** up the steep trail.
How did they climb? Carefully!

HOW MUCH?
They hiked **almost** all day.
How much? Did they hike all day? Almost!

Your Turn!
Use a pencil to write the answers on the blanks.

Later, they put up their tent.
When did they put up their tent? _____

Jampo put his dirty socks there.
Where did he put his socks? _____

The mountain goat quickly ate one sock.
How did the goat eat? _____

The goat ate nearly all of the other sock.
How much? Did it eat all of the other sock? _____

Adverbs Answer Questions

Lesson 7 Adverbs | PAGE 1

Adverbs Compare Verbs

*Adverbs are words used to **compare action verbs**.*

ONE ACTION
Adverbs compare one action.

The mountain goat grabbed Kipu's backpack.
It ran **fast**. It jumped **quickly** over rocks.

TWO ACTIONS
Adverbs compare two actions.

Kipu chased the goat.
The goat ran **faster** than Kipu.
It jumped **more quickly** over rocks than Kipu did.

THREE OR MORE ACTIONS
Adverbs compare three or more actions.

Kipu and Jampo chased the goat.
The goat ran the **fastest** of all.
It jumped over the rocks the **most quickly** of all.

DID YOU KNOW?
Adverbs that compare two actions end in –-er or add the word more.

DID YOU KNOW?
Adverbs that compare three or more actions end in –-est or add the word most.

Your Turn!
Use a pencil to circle the correct adverb.

Jampo shouted **louder / loudest** than Kipu.

The goat jumped the **higher / highest** of all three.

Kipu sneaked up on the goat **more quietly / most quietly** than Jampo and rescued his backpack.

I Know Adverbs!

Adverbs describe verbs.
Each adverb tells us something different about the action.

Jampo slid **slowly** down a cliff.
Jampo slid **quickly** down a cliff.
Jampo slid **frantically** down a cliff.
Jampo slid **lazily** down a cliff.

The goat **playfully** butted the tent.
The goat **angrily** butted the tent.
The goat **cheerfully** butted the tent.
The goat **noisily** butted the tent.

DID YOU KNOW?
You can choose to use interesting and exciting adverbs when you write!

Your Turn!
Use a pencil to draw a line to connect each verb with an interesting adverb.

VERB	ADVERB
chase	loudly
slide	slowly
chew	carefully
jump	quickly
shout	quietly

I Know Adverbs!

ADVERBS *answer questions about verbs.*

WHEN?

The goat **always** eats socks.

WHERE?

The goat likes to sleep **upstairs** in his new home.

HOW?

The goat sneaks **quietly** under the blanket.

HOW MUCH?

The mountain goat **usually** hides in Jampo's bed.

You can choose interesting and exciting adverbs when you write!

Lesson 7 Adverbs | PAGE 4

Adverbs Compare

ADVERBS *are words that compare action verbs.*

EXAMPLES:

chew **fast**
chew **faster**
chew **fastest**

hiked **quickly**
hiked **more quickly**
hiked **most quickly**

CHANGING ADJECTIVES TO ADVERBS

*Add **-ly** to an adjective to make it an adverb.*

joyful + **-ly** = joyfully

neat + **-ly** = neatly

wise + **-ly** = wisely

Lists of Adverbs

*Look for **adverbs** everywhere! Here are some you will find.*

ADVERBS TELL WHEN

always	never
usually	sometimes
recently	later
often	next
yesterday	tomorrow

ADVERBS TELL WHERE

anywhere	everywhere
nowhere	somewhere
here	there
inside	outside
downstairs	upstairs

ADVERBS TELL HOW

carefully	carelessly
softly	loudly
eagerly	lazily
patiently	impatiently
kindly	angrily

ADVERBS TELL HOW MUCH

nearly	almost
briefly	continually
hardly	fully
scarcely	completely
mostly	totally

Your Turn!

Use a pencil to write your favorite adverbs on the blanks.

The goat ate Jampo's shoe _____.

Kipu fished _____ in a stream.

The twins _____ fried fish for breakfast.

Lists of Adverbs

Good or Well?

WELL
The word well *is an adverb.*
Use it to describe a verb.

Jampo painted the picture **well**.
Kipu sang the song **well**.
The goat whistled **well**.

GOOD
The word good *is an adjective.*
Use it to describe a noun.

The goat is a **good** goat…sometimes.
Kipu did a **good** job putting up the tent.
Jampo fried some **good** fish.

HOW DO YOU FEEL?
Use well *to talk about your health.*
Use good *to talk about other feelings.*

After eating the tin can, the goat did not feel **well**.

Jampo felt **good** that he caught a fish.

Your Turn!
Use a pencil to circle the correct word.

Yesterday, the goat was not sick. It felt **well / good**. Kipu felt **well / good** about taking the goat home with them. The twins hiked **well / good** as they traveled down the mountain. The goat did a **well / good** job carrying their tent on its back.

Changing Adjectives to Adverbs

*Just add -ly to an adjective and you can **change it into an adverb**!*

Adjective: *quiet*
The **quiet** mountain goat tiptoed up to the tent.
Adverb: *quietly*
The snow fell **quietly** on the mountain.

Adjective: *loud*
Jampo heard a **loud** noise.
Adverb: *loudly*
"Look!" he shouted **loudly**, pointing at something near the tent.

Adjective: *frightful*
"It looks like a **frightful** snow monster," cried Kipu.
Adverb: *frightfully*
The snow monster shook its fur **frightfully**, and the snow fell off.

Adjective: *excited*
"That's not an **excited** snow monster," Jampo said.
Adverb: *excitedly*
"It's the mountain goat," Jampo said **excitedly**.

DID YOU KNOW?
Many adjectives can be changed into adverbs.

Your Turn!
Use a pencil to write the adverbs on the blanks.

Adjectives   Adverbs

blind + -ly = _____

glad + -ly = _____

kind + -ly = _____

open + -ly = _____

polite + -ly = _____

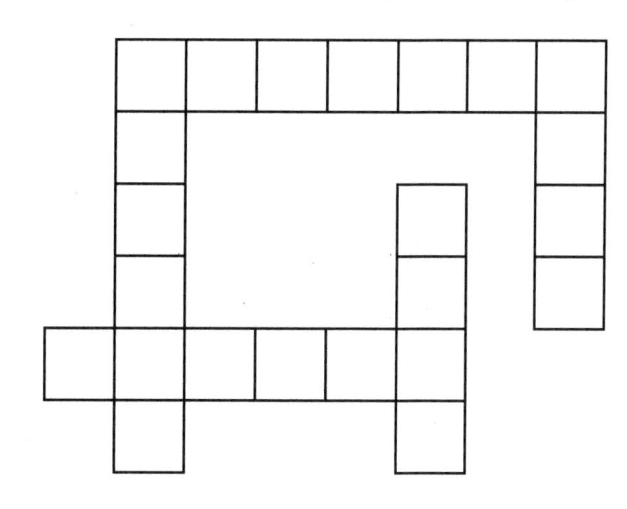

Prepositions Show Where

*Some **prepositions** give information about the location of something.*

WHERE?

above	in
across	near
against	off
among	on
around	outside
behind	over
below	through
beside	under
between	upon
by	with

Where did Jordan kick the soccer ball?
Jordan kicked the soccer ball **over** the goal.
Jordan kicked the soccer ball **behind** the goal.
Jordan kicked the soccer ball **beside** the goal.
Jordan kicked the soccer ball **inside** the goal.
Hooray! He scored a point!

Your Turn!

Use a pencil to put these prepositions into the word puzzle where they fit best.

behind
between
inside
near
over

Prepositions Show When

*Some **prepositions** give information about the time.*

WHEN?
after
before
by
during
past
since
till
to
until

When did Jordan kick the soccer ball?
Jordan kicked the ball **before** the game.
Jordan kicked the ball **after** the game.
Jordan kicked the ball **during** the game.
Hurrah! He scored another point!

Your Turn!
Use a pencil to write a preposition that shows WHEN in each space.

Jordan was hungry _____ the game started.

His mom passed out orange slices _____ halftime.

_____ the game, Jordan's team was having a pizza party.

He could hardly wait _____ then!

I Know Prepositions!

Prepositions are connecting words.
Prepositions connect nouns and pronouns with other words in a sentence.

PREPOSITIONS

across
against
along
down
from
into
off
onto
out of
toward
up

DID YOU KNOW?

Many prepositions describe movement.

Woof ran **onto** the soccer field.
Woof followed Jordan **down** the field.
Woof ran **into** the goal.
The goalie chased Woof **out of** the goal.
The referee chased Woof **off** the field.
Woof ran **toward** home.
Good-bye, Woof!

Your Turn!

Use a pencil to draw a line to connect each preposition with a noun to show movement.

PREPOSITION

against	the doghouse
along	the fence
toward	the house
down	the sidewalk
up	the street
into	the candy store

I Know Prepositions!

I Know Prepositions!

PREPOSITIONS *connect nouns and pronouns with other words in a sentence.*

Prepositions show movement.

along
down
into
toward

Prepositions show where.

behind
between
near
over

Prepositions show when.

after
before
during
until

Prepositional Phrases (sidebar)

A prepositional phrase is a group of words that starts with a preposition.

inside the doghouse
toward the doghouse
beside the doghouse

before the game
during the game
after the game

around the goal
behind the goal
into the goal

DID YOU KNOW?

A preposition is always the first word in a prepositional phrase.

Prepositional Phrases

A **prepositional phrase** is a group of words that starts with a preposition.

Woof napped **inside the doghouse**.
Where did Woof nap?
inside the doghouse

Woof ran **toward the doghouse**.
How did Woof move?
toward the doghouse

Woof buried a bone **beside the doghouse**.
Where did Woof bury his bone?
beside the doghouse

DID YOU KNOW?
A preposition is always the first word in a prepositional phrase.

Your Turn!
Use a pencil to write the prepositional phrase on the blanks.

Woof dug a hole in the field.

_____ _____ _____

Then he chased Jordan around the tree.

_____ _____ _____

Woof ran under the bleachers.

_____ _____ _____

Woof misbehaved at the soccer game.

_____ _____

_____ _____

Prepositional Phrases as Adverbs

*Some **prepositional phrases are used as adverbs**.
They describe verbs.*

played **during the rain**
Jordan's soccer team played during the rain.

slid **toward the referee**
Jordan slipped and slid toward the referee.

flew **past the goalie**
He kicked the ball, and it flew past the goalie.

Jordan's team won the game. Hooray!

Your Turn!
*Use a pencil to underline the prepositional phrase in this sentence.
Then draw a picture to show how the prepositional phrase describes the verb.*

Jordan grabbed his trophy, jumped in the air, and cheered!

Capitalization

Capital letters are an important part of writing.

Writers can use lower case letters like **a, b, c** or capital letters like **A, B, C**.

Lower Case Letters
a b c d e f g h i j k l m n o p q r s t u v w x y z

Capital Letters
A B C D E F G H I J K L M N O P Q R S T U V W X Y Z

Capitalization means to use a capital letter when you write.

DID YOU KNOW?
There are important rules about using capital letters.

DID YOU KNOW?
For most capitalization rules, only use a capital letter for the first letter in the word.

Incorrect
CAPTAIN PEGLEG

Correct
Captain **P**egleg

Your Turn!
Use a pencil to capitalize the following words, and write each word correctly on the blank line.

ohio: _____

july: _____

ryan: _____

saturn: _____

Titles

*Capitalize the first word, the last word, and every important word in **titles** of books, magazines, newspapers, songs, poems, and movies, even if the word is short.*

The pirate captain chose the book ***How** to **R**ead a **T**reasure **M**ap*.

The pirate crew watched the movie ***D**anger on the **S**even **S**eas*.

The cabin boy read the book ***L**earn to **B**e a **P**irate*.

"**B**low the **M**an **D**own" is the crew's favorite sea song.

DID YOU KNOW?
Unless it is the first word, do not capitalize little words in titles. Little words can include:

a, an, the, but, as, if, and, or, nor

The cook's parrot enjoyed watching the movie ***A** Cracker for Polly*.

Captain Pegleg recited the poem "**T**he Sea and I."

The first mate read the book ***A** Tale of Two Pirates*.

Your Turn!
Underline each of the following book titles that is capitalized correctly.

It's a Pirate's Life for Me

How To Use A Compass For Beginning Pirates

A Pirate's Parrot is his Best Friend

Recipes for a Pirate Cook

Capitalization Rules

ABBREVIATIONS
Use capital letters when writing many shorter forms of long words or phrases such as abbreviations, acronyms, or official titles.

Mr. Salty
TV
Sen. Snooks

TITLES
Capitalize the first word, the last word, and every important word in titles of books, magazines, newspapers, songs, poems, and movies, even if they are short.

***D**anger on the **S**even **S**eas*

PROPER NOUNS
Capitalize the first letter of proper nouns.

Squawk
June
Hawaii

Capitalize adjectives that come from proper nouns.

Chinese food

Capitalization Rules

SENTENCES
Write a capital letter to start the first word at the beginning of every sentence.

The cook's parrot hid inside a crackerbarrel.

He ate all the crackers!

QUOTES
When quotations are used, use a capital letter to start the first word of the speaker's sentence inside the quotes.

The pirate captain asked, "**Where** be the cook's parrot?"

LETTERS
Use capital letters when writing certain parts of a letter.

Abbreviations

*Use capital letters when writing many shorter forms of long words or phrases such as **abbreviations**, acronyms, or official titles.*

Abbreviations
Mister Salty is the first mate.
Mr. Salty is the first mate.

He bought a parrot on Broad Street.
He bought a parrot on Broad **St.**

Acronyms
The pirate crew watched television.
The pirate crew watched **TV**.

Captain Pegleg is a member of the International Pirate Association.
Captain Pegleg is a member of the **IPA**.

Official Titles
First aboard ship was Senator Snooks.
First aboard ship was **Sen.** Snooks.

Your Turn!
Use a pencil to draw a line that connects each abbreviation or acronym with the word or phrase it stands for.

DOB	avenue
Jan.	doctor
Ave.	United States of America
Jr.	date of birth
USA	junior
Dr.	Kentucky Fried Chicken®
KFC	January

Sentences

*Write a capital letter to start the first word at the beginning of every **sentence**.*

The pirate captain and his crew set sail for the Seven Seas.
They followed the treasure map for three weeks.
Storms tossed their ship about, but they kept a steady course.
Finally, they arrived at the spot where the buried treasure was located on the map.
But this was no desert island with sand and palm trees!
This place was covered with snow and ice.

DID YOU KNOW?
When quotations are used, start the first word of the speaker's sentence inside the quotes with a capital letter.

The pirate captain shouted, "**Methinks** we have the wrong treasure map!"

Your Turn!
Use the capitalization proofreading symbol from your Self-editing Fold-N-Go to mark the first letter at the beginning of every sentence. Write the correct capital letter above.

the first mate spoke up, "but Captain! that is the proper treasure map. there must be buried treasure around here somewhere." at this news, the pirate crew grabbed snow shovels. they dug for buried treasure in the snow. finally, their shovels hit something. it was a treasure chest! they opened it up, but it was filled with ice cream bars. "aargh!" cried the pirate captain. "there be trickery afoot!"

Dictionary

*A **dictionary** tells us important information about words.*

SPELLING
Use a dictionary to look up the correct spelling of a word.

DID YOU KNOW?
*Each word in a dictionary is called an **Entry Word**.*

PRONUNCIATION
Use a dictionary to see how to pronounce a new word.
A dictionary has a pronunciation key on each page to help you.

SYLLABLES
Use a dictionary to check how a word is divided into syllables.

DEFINITION
Use a dictionary to discover the meaning of a word.

PARTS OF SPEECH
A dictionary lists whether a word is a noun, verb, adjective, or other part of speech. It also gives examples to show how to use the word in a sentence.

DID YOU KNOW?
*At the top of each page in a dictionary you'll find the **Guide Words**.*
Guide Words are the first and last word on that page.

WORD FORMS
A dictionary lists different forms of the same word such as *happy, happier,* and *happiest.*

DID YOU KNOW?
Many words have more than one meaning.
A dictionary lists the different meanings of each word.

Your Turn!
Look up the word invention *in a dictionary. Then use a pencil and write the answers to these questions.*

1. How many syllables does *invention* have? _____

2. What part of speech is *invention*? _____

Thesaurus

*A **thesaurus** is a special kind of dictionary that groups words with similar meanings together in a list. A thesaurus helps us choose strong words to replace weak words.*

ALPHABETICAL ORDER
Just like a dictionary, a thesaurus lists words in alphabetical order from A to Z.

DID YOU KNOW?
Sometimes, instead of listing words in alphabetical order, a thesaurus might list words according to categories such as "furniture" and "fruits."

SYNONYMS
A thesaurus lists *synonyms*, or words that mean the same as the entry word.

A synonym for *happy* is **cheerful**.

ANTONYMS
A thesaurus lists *antonyms*, or words that mean the opposite of the entry word.

An antonym for *happy* is **gloomy**.

PARTS OF SPEECH
A thesaurus states whether a word is a noun, verb, adjective, or other part of speech.

DID YOU KNOW?
A thesaurus does not give the definition, or meaning, of words. If you find a word in a thesaurus that you want to use, first look it up in the dictionary to check what it means.

Your Turn!
Look up these words in a thesaurus. Then use a pencil to write two synonyms for each word.

invention: _____ _____

build: _____ _____

idea: _____ _____

References

*Writers use key **reference** materials to help them write better.*

DICTIONARY
Use a dictionary to look up information about words.

Jared saw a sign in town. The sign said:
Contest! Build a New Contrivance!
"What's a contrivance?" Liliana asked.
"I don't know," Jared said.
They looked up the word in a **dictionary**.
It meant something that is made.

THESAURUS
Use a thesaurus to find other words that mean the same thing.

"Let's find more words that mean the same thing," Jared said.
They looked up *contrivance* in a **thesaurus**.
"It's an invention!" Liliana said. "I want to build a new invention."
"I do, too!" replied Jared.

ENCYCLOPEDIA
Use an encyclopedia to find lots of information about something.

"Let's learn more about inventions," Jared said.
They looked up *invention* in an **encyclopedia**.
They learned many things and found plenty of ideas.

Your Turn!
Use a pencil to write down these references after you unscramble the letters in each word.

coineyplaced: _____

shauteurs: _____

trainycoid: _____

References

Writers use key reference materials to help them write better.

DICTIONARY

Use a dictionary to look up information about words.

THESAURUS

Use a thesaurus to find other words that mean the same thing.

ENCYCLOPEDIA

Use an encyclopedia to find lots of information about something.

INTERNET

Use the Internet to look up information about a variety of topics.

LIBRARY

Use the library to find books to gather research.

Dictionary

A dictionary tells us important information about words.

SPELLING

Use a dictionary to look up the correct spelling of a word.

PRONUNCIATION

Use a dictionary to see how to pronounce a new word.

SYLLABLES

Use a dictionary to check how a word is divided into syllables.

DEFINITION

Use a dictionary to discover the meaning of a word.

PARTS OF SPEECH

A dictionary lists whether a word is a noun, verb, adjective, or other part of speech.

More References

*Writers use **more references** to help them write better.*

INTERNET
Use the Internet to look up information about a variety of topics.

"I want to see what kinds of inventions kids are building right now all around the world," Jared said. "Maybe we'll get even more ideas."
"Let's search on the **Internet**," Liliana suggested.

LIBRARY
Use the library to find books to gather research.

"Let's invent a flying machine," Liliana said.
"Great idea!" Jared exclaimed.
"First, let's read how they invented the airplane," said Liliana.
"Okay," said Jared. "They have a book about that at the **library**."

LIST YOUR REFERENCES
When you write, be sure to make a list of website addresses, titles of books, and names of magazines or encyclopedia articles that you use for your research.

DID YOU KNOW?
*To find the closest library that has a certain book, look on **www.WorldCat.org**.*

Your Turn!
Use a pencil to write your answers to these questions.

1. Which reference would you use to look up the meaning of a word? _____

2. Which reference would you use to see if anything was invented this month? _____

3. Which reference would you use to find three books about famous inventors? _____

More References

Internet

*The **Internet** has become an important reference.*

DID YOU KNOW?
You can find a free dictionary, thesaurus, and encyclopedia to use on the Internet.

www.dictionary.com
www.thesaurus.com
www.factmonster.com

SEARCH
Use the Internet to search for key words.
Type the key words into a search engine search box.
Press ***enter***. A list of websites will appear that are related to your key words.

URL
The address of a website is called its URL. When you type in the URL, you can go directly to the website. URLs usually start with **http://** or **www.**

DID YOU KNOW?
Not every site on the Internet has accurate information. Try to find websites that look like they are from official organizations.

DID YOU KNOW?
Be careful when you use the Internet. Some websites are not safe. Always ask a trusted grown-up for help, and follow your family's Internet safety rules.

Your Turn!
Use a pencil to circle the correct answers.

1. What is the address of a website?   VFW   URL   AAA

2. Is every website safe to explore?   Yes   No

3. Every website has accurate information.   True   False

Encyclopedia

*An **encyclopedia** is a large reference that contains many articles on different topics.*

"I want to learn more about inventions," Liliana said. "I would like to know who famous inventors are. I'm curious about inventions from long ago. I want to discover more about inventions from different countries."

"We have a set of encyclopedias at our house," Jared said. "Let's use them to learn more."

ALPHABETICAL ORDER
Most encyclopedias arrange topics in alphabetical order from A to Z.

DID YOU KNOW?
An encyclopedia can be one book, a set of books, a computer program, or a website on the Internet.

ARTICLES
Different entries in an encyclopedia are called **articles**.
Usually, each article has a **title**.
Each article is often written by a different **author** whose name is listed with the article.

CROSS-REFERENCES
Many articles list other articles within the encyclopedia where you can look to find more about your topic.

INDEX
Most encyclopedias have an index so that you can search where to find information about your topic.

DID YOU KNOW?
When you list a reference from an encyclopedia, write down the name of the encyclopedia, the title of the article, and the name of its author if you know it. It is also important to develop the habit of writing down the copyright date and page numbers.

Your Turn!
Use a pencil to write the answers to the following questions after you look up information in an encyclopedia.

1. Who invented crayons? _____

2. Who invented the paperclip? _____

3. Who invented root beer? _____

Answer Key

Level 1 Fold-N-Go™ Grammar Pack
Remove Answer Key and store in a notebook or folder

Lesson 1 - Punctuation Marks

Page 1: Periods

    Mr. Marino is taking us to Pirate Bay on Saturday. We are going to hunt for Captain Jack's treasure. Landon and T.C. will be there. I hope you will come too. Bring $6.95 for lunch. Find out about Pirate Bay at www.PirateBayTreasure.com.

Page 2: Exclamation Points

Stop! Don't open the treasure chest!
We get all the gold! Hip, hip, hooray!

Page 3: Question Marks

What time is it?
Where do you live?

Page 4: Quotation Marks

Captain Jack asked, "Who stole my gold?"
I'm writing a story called "Pirate's Gold."

Page 5: Apostrophes

(You're) invited to (Tommy's) campfire!
(We'll) toast marshmallows over the fire.
(We're) meeting at the (Children's) center.

Page 6: Commas

                        May 17, 2014

Dear Grandpa,

    I went to a dinosaur museum in Blanding, Utah. Lucy, my neighbor, had never been there before. She loved it! We saw fossils, skeletons, and footprints. There was a gift shop, and we bought postcards. Later, we had a picnic at a shady, beautiful park. Lucy and I had a lot of fun.

                        Your grandson,
                        Henry

Lesson 2 - Self-editing

Page 1: Content

Superheroes know that power-packed writing has:
A strong **beginning**.
A developed **middle**.
A satisfying **end**.

Page 2: Self-editing Check

The marks I make on my paper to correct my mistakes are called **proofreading marks**.

I look in a **dictionary** to check my spelling, and I look in a **thesaurus** to find strong words.

Page 3: Proofreading Marks A

superball Girl bounces over hills. Eraser Kid turns every thing invisible.They they are amazing.

Page 4: Proofreading Marks B

Superheroes look for babies, children, and grandmas to help.

"Help," cries Julio.

Page 5: Self-editing Tools

Answers will vary.

Page 6: Self-editing Tips

Answers will vary.

Lesson 3 - Nouns

Page 1: I Know Nouns!

Answers will vary. Make sure at least one answer is a proper noun.

Page 2: Common and Proper Nouns

Answers will vary. Each answer must be a proper noun and begin with a capital letter.

Page 3: Collective Nouns

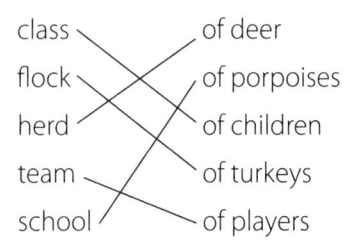

class — of children
flock — of turkeys
herd — of deer
team — of players
school — of porpoises

Level 1 Answer Key | PAGE 3

Page 4: Plural Nouns: Add -s or -es

Jessica and Noah are junior **astronauts**. They grab their **helmets** out of their **boxes**. They pull on their **gloves** and pack their **lunches**. Now they are ready to blast off and plant two **flags** on Pluto!

Page 5: Plural Nouns: Change the Letter

Jessica and Noah write in their (diaries).
On their trip, they are bringing three (guppies).
The (shelves) inside the rocket are full.

Page 6: Plural Nouns: Irregular

Jessica and Noah have two (sheep) inside the rocket.
Three (mice) have sneaked on board.
Jessica and Noah will be the first (children) to walk on Pluto!

Lesson 4 - Pronouns

Page 1: I Know Pronouns!

She told **them** it was a wishing tree.
It could grow bikes and toys and candy.
It could grow **anything they** wished!

Page 2: Singular or Plural Pronouns

Tatum gave candy bars to all (her) friends.
Bryant ate (his) candy bar right away.
Tatum's friends ate (their) candy bars, too.

Page 3: Male or Female Pronouns

Rhiannon planted (her) seed. A giant wishing tree grew up in (her) back yard. The President took **his** seed back to the White House. **He** planted the seed in **his** yard. **He** soon had a giant wishing tree, too.

Page 4: Jobs Pronouns Do

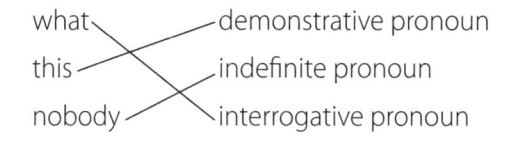

what — interrogative pronoun
this — demonstrative pronoun
nobody — indefinite pronoun

Page 5: Personal Pronouns

em = **me**   rhe = **her**   etyh = **they**
oyu = **you**   eh = **he**   esh = **she**

Page 6: Possessive Pronouns

These are (her) seeds.
This is (our) bush.
Special fruit grew on (its) branches.

Lesson 5 - Verbs

Page 1: Action Verbs

Tater Alligator **digs** up tiny potatoes from the field.
He **grabs** potatoes at the restaurant.
All day long, he **chomps** on potatoes.

Page 2: Present Tense Verbs

Tater Alligator **stomps** into the restaurant.
He **nibbles** all the french fries.
Tater Alligator **looks** for sweet potatoes, too.

Page 3: Linking Verbs

Potatoes **are** a problem for Tater Alligator.
He **has been** greedy. Now he **is** too big for his overalls.
They **were** the right size last week, but now they **are** too tight.
If he **is** not careful, soon he **will be** too big for his favorite pajamas.

Page 4: Past Tense Regular Verbs

D	W	B	A	R	K	E	D	D	X
E	T	Z	A	Q	Y	Z	O	E	M
C	L	E	A	N	E	D	L	P	A
N	R	J	D	E	P	P	O	P	R
A	X	O	Z	O	W	D	Q	O	C
D	O	Q	W	Y	E	J	X	H	H
D	E	N	E	P	O	T	R	Y	E
W	Q	I	M	A	G	I	N	E	D
H	X	U	Z	Y	X	R	W	B	F
K	J	G	L	A	U	G	H	E	D

Page 5: Past Tense Irregular Verbs

Last week, Brandon **taught** Tater Alligator a new trick.
Tater Alligator **sat** on command.
Then Brandon **fed** him a french fry for a reward.

Page 6: Future Tense Verbs

will try
will count
will lift
will skip
Tater **T o t s** ®

Lesson 6 - Adjectives

Page 1: Where Adjectives Are Found

nervous, eager, sly, lovely

Page 2: Adjectives Compare Things

Kirk's hat is (**taller**) than Craig's.
Mariah's tutu is the (**most pink**) of all.
Mariah dances the (**longest**) dance of all.

Page 3: I Know Adjectives!

Answers will vary.

Page 4: Lists of Adjectives

Answers will vary.

Page 5: Using Adjectives When We Write

Kirk does get a (**new**) coat, but it is (**baggier**) than his (**old**) coat.
He's (**grumpy**) because he can't find the (**perfect**) coat.

Page 6: Using Adjectives in Poetry

Answers will vary.

Lesson 7 - Adverbs

Page 1: Adverbs Answer Questions

Later, there, quickly, nearly

Page 2: Adverbs Compare Verbs

Jampo shouted (**louder**) than Kipu.
The goat jumped the (**highest**) of all three.
Kipu sneaked up on the goat (**more quietly**) than Jampo.

Page 3: I Know Adverbs!

Answers will vary.

Page 4: Lists of Adverbs

Answers will vary.

Page 5: Good or Well?

Yesterday, the goat was not sick. It felt (**well**).
Kipu felt (**good**) about taking the goat home with them.
The twins hiked (**well**) as they traveled down the mountain.
The goat did a (**good**) job carrying their tent on its back.

Page 6: Changing Adjectives to Adverbs

blindly, gladly, kindly, openly, politely

Lesson 8 - Prepositions

Page 1: Prepositions Show Where

	B	E	T	W	E	E	N
	E						E
	H			O			A
	I			V			R
I	N	S	I	D	E		
	D			R			

Page 2: Prepositions Show When

Answers may vary. Suggested answers include:

Jordan was hungry **before** the soccer game.
His mom passed out orange slices **during** halftime.
After the game, the team planned a pizza party.
Jordan could hardly wait **till** (or **until**) then.

Page 3: I Know Prepositions!

Answers will vary.

Page 4: Prepositional Phrases

in the field
around the tree
under the bleachers
at the soccer game

Page 5: Prepositional Phrases as Adjectives

Student should draw a picture to illustrate ONE of the following prepositional phrases:

Woof tasted the fries **in the brown bag**. *(Drawing should show a dog with his nose in a bag.)*
A dog **with a blue collar** saw Woof eating fries. *(Drawing should show a dog wearing a blue collar.)*

Page 6: Prepositional Phrases as Adverbs

Jordan grabbed his trophy, jumped **in the air**, and cheered!
(Drawing should show a boy jumping in the air.)

Lesson 9 - Capitalization

Page 1: Capitalization
Ohio, July, Ryan, Saturn

Page 2: Proper Nouns
(Squawk) likes to ride around on (Jim's) shoulder. Every (morning), (Squawk) plays a game of (Chinese checkers) with the (crew). He dreams of traveling to the (Empire State Building) one day.

Page 3: Titles
It's a Pirate's Life for Me
Recipes for a Pirate Cook

Page 4: Abbreviations
DOB — date of birth
Jan. — January
Ave. — avenue
Jr. — junior
USA — United States of America
Dr. — doctor
KFC — Kentucky Fried Chicken®

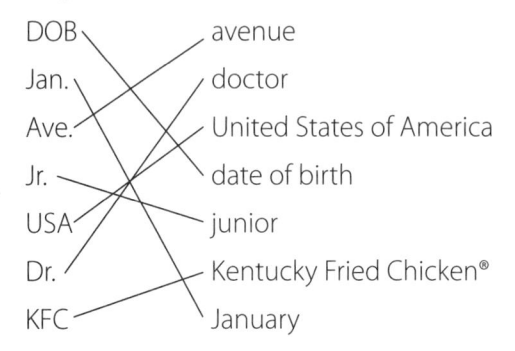

Page 5: Letters

                                          Wednesday, **M**ay 2

Dear ship's mates,
      It be time to clean up the pirate ship. Swab the decks! Mend the sails! All hands will report on deck tomorrow morning at sunrise.

                                          Yer captain,
                                          Pegleg

Page 6: Sentences
    The first mate spoke up, "**B**ut Captain! **T**hat is the proper treasure map. **T**here must be buried treasure around here somewhere." **A**t this news, the pirate crew grabbed snow shovels. **T**hey dug for buried treasure in the snow. **F**inally, their shovels hit something. **I**t was a treasure chest! **T**hey opened it up, but it was filled with ice cream bars. "**A**argh!" cried the pirate captain. "**T**here be trickery afoot!"

Lesson 10 - References

Page 1: Dictionary

How may syllables does *invention* have? 3
What part of speech is *invention?* noun

Page 2: Thesaurus

Answers will vary.

Page 3: References

encyclopedia
thesaurus
dictionary

Page 4: More References

Answers may vary, but suggested answers include:

1. encyclopedia
2. thesaurus
3. dictionary

Page 5: Internet

1. URL
2. No
3. False

Page 6: Encyclopedia

1. Who invented crayons? Edwin Binney and C. Harold Smith
2. Who invented the paperclip? Johan Vaaler
3. Who invented root beer? Charles Hires